MAIDEN NAMES

REMEDIA AMORIS

In reaching past the loss of love,
both hands play their part;
one to jettison old hope,
one to close the heart.

To Catherine,

a big night in westport!

MAIDEN NAMES

with best wishes —

Martin Dyar

ARLEN
HOUSE

This 2nd edition of
MAIDEN NAMES

is published in 2015 by
ARLEN HOUSE
42 Grange Abbey Road
Baldoyle
Dublin 13
Ireland
Phone/Fax: 353 86 8207617
Email: arlenhouse@gmail.com
arlenhouse.blogspot.com

Distributed internationally by
SYRACUSE UNIVERSITY PRESS
621 Skytop Road, Suite 110
Syracuse, NY 13244–5290
Phone: 315–443–5534/Fax: 315–443–5545
Email: supress@syr.edu
syracuseuniversitypress.syr.edu

ISBN 978–1–85132–123–0, paperback

Typesetting: Arlen House
Printed lithographically in Ireland
Cover Image: 'Inland' by Martin Gale
1984, oil on canvas, 106 x 106cm
www.martingale.ie

CONTENTS

To Paddy and Valerie

MAIDEN NAMES

DOCTOR FOSTER

In your mother's time Foster was at his best.
He'd come to town, once, maybe twice a year,
a bulging, bearded figure, full of life.

He'd always been the warts and depression man,
effective with his similar approach to both.
Only in later years – market forces –

did he style himself a pregnancy guru.
It stung me, but from the gate I'd watch the clinic:
local women assembling in the sun,

and Foster there regaling them, guffawing
in shared delight when told a previous
pain had passed, performing bashfulness

if someone brought a gift. In the end, love
drove me to dream of staging a disgrace
of the man. That shrewd womb-tinkering air

would no longer leave me picturing my girls
signed up to feel the body's hold on the heart
made less in a fabulous afternoon of trust.

THE GROUP SCHEME

You carry these things. I knew the house
in question was the home of a lad drowned
in the Moy in the sixties, and that his
mother had not eaten fish since that day;
they never found a body, the divers, and
I knew she lived alone, though I couldn't
think of her name. But you carry these things.
'I'm two days without water,' Mrs Burke
told me. Burke, that's it. I apologised.
I said pipes elsewhere were giving hassle
and that I'd have a look, tide her over
for the weekend, whatever the problem.
She was firm but chatty, and intrigued
that Callow Lake fed this village and more.
'A farty enough source, for the whole district
to be washing and drinking and the rest,
cattle and cars and windows and what have you.'
'And is it filtered?' she wanted to know.
'There'll be a brand new system going in.'
Her reply to this was cool: 'Ours is not
modern so. Is it even good to drink?'
'It's grand for tea,' I said, invoking tea
as blesser of our nerves, and to eclipse
with wryness the two days she'd been without.
Then I spoke about the purifying sand
and stone system that we had at the *point
of extraction* for years, sidling here
for terms that might downplay the blackness,
the volume of the lake. But now the hole
I'd dug at her door was like my own mind's eye.
It needed work. I strove for greater tact
and less awareness welling in my brain.
She watched me strike the pipes. I sensed
then a son beneath us, sinking or waiting,

disturbed and now dislodged. 'Do I know your
people?' she asked. 'Aren't you Doherty?'
'I am,' I said, fiercer now with the hammer.
'Your father did the search and recovery
for years,' she said. 'He did,' I said. 'God bless
him,' she said. And I couldn't get over her
warmth. My breath was short, in sympathy,
my gut all tight, suspicious of the job.

THE JOY OF CARDS

I'm ninety-four, but I tend to say
that I am younger by ten years.
It quells the astonishment of some.

Twice every week, I travel by bus
to play cards in Cricklewood.
I wouldn't have this rhythm questioned

and I don't like being reminded
that perhaps I should be frailer than I am.
If doubt occurs, I picture time.

There's nothing surer than time's love.
In the joy of a card night, it's there:
hosts of summers summoning me still.

And, anyway, it's far too easily felt
these days that one has lived too long.
'I'm in my eighties,' I say, my tone

informative, cautiously warm,
into the ear of whoever is curious,
no echo of what this world makes of life.

We'd been wondering, and then a text explained:
'Affairs. On both sides. Wedding off.' But then
that night it was all back on. The same sister
revealed: 'They're both gutted, but marrying still.'

If you knew Margaret and Tony, you'd appreciate
what a fine circle ours was to roll with their guff.
Both consistently bullied their confidantes.
Both were volubly prudish, obstreperously vain.

We were a fine circle, but not so absolute
in our friendships as not to welcome the valve
of this misfortune. And so we texted each other
furtively for days, astounded either had found
another to bear the hooves of their personality,
and thrilled the big day now would have such themes.

Lads, know this. The name *Jennifer*
confines a man to endless festivals.
Just as the lilt of *Elizabeth* sets him
up for months of email typing.

Let these reports form a wisdom,
a means to predict the lovely snare.
I've known numerous *Jennifers*.
Each, in her happiness, wrecked me.

My *Elizabeths*, one a *Betty*, were
chatty, British, unmarryable greats.
But the name *Deirdre* is fiercest.
A stellar fuse brought this name about,

a global ghost whistling vastly,
the owl of the earth coining a new dawn.
Brothers. The ancient, propulsive,
and far too musical grace of *Deirdre*,

whatever powers of love or praise
you'll use against her, will not end.

INDEPENDENCE

His mother and his sisters gave up on him
in his forties. There were admirers in the town,
opportunities in Galway and Dublin,
yet doggedly he built his vintage solitude.

And even in the years when the odd echo
of his origins could reach him still, in the dawn
of his middle-age loneliness, he persevered.
Suicide spoke, but he'd the same deafness ready.

Lately though, at night, his blood gathers itself
against that will. It ladles across his mind
an early vanity: memories of being wanted,
memories, some fictive, of being silver-tongued.
While his heart, a kind of fox, climbs down to the lake
and begs the dark to strike or bless the cottage.

The job they're given is fairly simple.
Find the place,
go in for half an hour and discuss the settlement.
Consider, if it's appropriate,
the few antiques: the safe,
the signs, the switchboard.
Glance at the books, the electrics.
Perhaps fill out some forms.
But these aul' ones, these Cathleens, these Annies,
they can be fierce long-winded.
For some of our lads their ways
are just too compelling.

Some accept a drink, some'll have lunch.
We'd a Polish guy who took
a ninety-two-year-old out in the van.
She showed him a ball alley.
Fair enough: dozens of ghosts
and no graffiti. But if you're not direct
about the job? You understand,
we've had to weed out the dreamers.
Immunity to stories, I find,
is the primary quality.
You don't want to be sitting at an old table,
under a clock that strikes you

as fabulously loud.
Or find yourself cradled by the past,
thinking a man need venture
no further west than the brink he meets
in a mouthful of milky tea.
If the archive-harbouring frailty
of the postmistress soothes you;
if her wit grants you the lost farm

and maternity of the world;
if her isolated, dwindling village, a place
without a pub or a shop,
whose nearest decent-sized

town is itself desperately quiet –
if these things move you ...
What I mean is, if you can't meet
a forgotten countryside
head on, and calmly dismantle her,
fold her up, carry her out,
and ship her back
to Head Office, however ambiguous,
however heavy-handed or fateful,
however bloody poignant
the whole affair might seem to you;
if you can't stand your ground

when a steep moment
of hospitable chat and reminiscence
might tempt you to put
your mobile phone on silent,
or worse, blinded by plates of fruit cake,
to switch it off completely;
if you cannot accompany
an inevitable change, knowing
you did not cause these people, these ways, to vanish,
and if you will not sign off
on expired things for us,
then, I'm sorry, but you are not our man.

You'll be hearing about me when you visit.
In town they'll describe me as mad in the head.
And I suppose I might've earned that judgment.
Yes, I stole the sign for Cloonygowan Stone Fort
three times, battling for years with the Council
and never once replying to them. But your friends
the gossipers cannot imagine my contentment,
up there for hours, preening the fort, weeding her,
sunk in energetic silence, fixing the pathways
the tourists won't use. How could those people,
having branded me a queerhawk, a bollocks
or a looney, how could they come to appreciate
my good days, the changeable weather lighting
my work, my afternoons shielded and primed
by limestone time sealed in but still affirming
a misanthropic wealth at the heart of things?
Dear visitor, when your hosts point me out,
as you drive down one of our several hundred
remarkable boreens, and I'm there with my collie
on the glossy verge, in sunlight, scythe in hand,
framed by thorns and flowers, as I mostly am,
and if the stories told serve to quicken the thrum
of Ireland on your nerves, leaving you unable
to tune in to sounds beyond the voice of the town
conveying with cold humour the quizzical threat
of a solitary farmer, a loveless man who had only
his mother, all his faceless sisters dead in Leeds,
and if they speak of the last time I was seen jarred,
getting into bother, two years ago, on Fair Day,
my stoical dogs at the copshop gate next morning –
Well, my friend, you're welcome to the legend
and to your slant on the pain and the peace behind it.
But if I don't salute you as you pass, minding
my step, as your jeep berates the tangled ditches,

and you travel into Callow, Lismorane, Toomore
and Renbrack (I'll meet no other traffic that day)
and if, as I vanish, you're rooting for your camera,
convinced my face, like nothing else, bespeaks
old Mayo – if I'm your bog icon, then good luck.
Your towny guides are leading you astray.

THE HEIFER'S YES

The earth, I know, requires
the substance of this torpor.
Over time, winding
among ancestors, she found
this, me, a kind of girl.
I have these nettles.
I have this reappearing day.
I have these boulders
and the vitality of my coughing.
I have too the spirit wheel
that is the will to graze.
The earth, rooting my life,
granted me, lovingly,
this love for heavy rain,
and if my tongue was rooted less
I might try to praise her:
Hill, Grandmother, hold my skull
closer to your own.

TIN WHISTLE

The mandolins
of the rookeries
have strewn
their loud,
anointing pressures
upon me.
I listen now
to the wet trees,
now to the women.
Two coastal
rhythms,
two laughters
galvanising
the labour of the tune.
I am old
but I approach
by such possession
my fulfilment.

IN THERE

The swollen mare, an animate hillside dolmen,
was the warmest thing in the field.
In the rain we approached her
with the vet who would insert his arm
into the tight cave of her life,
under her tail, in there, where I imagined
tongues of Braille-flesh spoke things on his hand
that my parents paid him to translate.

And I could not imagine her insides as dark.
I thought there had to be something there,
clearer than daylight, the stuff and the place
so profound to be said of, *life comes from*.
She groaned but stood still, an inconvenienced
yet tolerant oracle in our inquiring midst.

Sunk to his shoulder in hot equine encasement,
the vet fixed his eye on the distance and read.
And then, the check-up complete, his sheathed arm
glistening with the grease of horse health,
he smoked and spoke to my parents.

With the sight of the mare's soaked oak neck,
big veins there like suede worms,
my eight year old mind pulsed,
her mane of treacle laces, her bulbous inky eyes,
maternal in ways that made me feel safe and sad.

Drizzle drifted through
where steam from her body met
our visible breaths,
two clouds of creaturely presence
diffusing together in February light.

Pleased, we descended the hill,
my ankles weak upon the hoof craters,
the Lilliputian castles of manure
unmade by Mayo weather; the rain
falling steadily upon
the ocean of sympathy that was
that sacred word, *foal*.

Tumgesh Witches

Margaret, studying the magpies.
Joan, gone quiet with her sense of the fox.
Imelda, selecting nettles and whistling.

Jude, crouched down, eyeballing an insect wing.
Ursula, consumed by the speed of the streams.
Lorraine, addressing restlessly the mountains.

Kate, black from venturing underground.
Maeve, wandering again from her duties.
Bairbre, at the cave mouth, calling *sisters*.

DIVINITY AND HARE

I stayed with her because she seemed unwell.
You could wait, I said, and choose another form,
some other creature, another time or means.
You needn't send yourself into this change.
But though she was a being full of doubt,
there at the stream, at the field's edge, she stood
and made her mind a door to the heart of the hare.
And then, as gods in this mode sometimes do,
she conjured for herself a kind of breath
and spat divine reluctance to the ground.
And summer seemed to take this as a cue:
the field smells were a sunlit channel now
and walls of birds eclipsed my last advice
to her, timid, transformed, hell bent on life.

THE SOUTERRAIN NUN

There will always be talk of the human mine.
Talk of what we truly are. A route suggesting,
though it is not life, a home in the elements.
Many have scraped their way down to paradise,

conditioned to take from their own fatigue
a drop of beckoning which serves to spur them on.
I have long dreamt of that metamorphic
patience in those anonymous sufferers.

And that will be me. Digger. Mineral saint.
I know that I will thrive as a spirit of drainage,
that I can outswim incarnation, returning,
when she speaks with my pain, a limestone curse:

You are not what I am now, beneath you,
flint-eyed, alert, amphibiously reborn.

AISLING HILL

You, who too infrequently choose a farmer,
seizing and drenching his work-scented body,
only to return him at dawn to the laws of nature.
You must know these broken men recall you.

And that accidental witnesses they were not
but men who'd sought you long, as I seek you,
alone from moon to moon, and muttering piously:
'O my lady of the thrice-derelict cottage.

My lady of gorse.' Have you not, discretest
apparition, heard the tunes we've played
in plucky efforts to have you from the stars?
Or is spirit a tool that fails you when you crouch
at the dream we trappers of miracle must chase,
bidding the taste of your foliage and your light?

THE TIMONEY BELL

There's a dream that comes to me around March.
I'll have been thinking about the bell, the ceremony,
the singular depth of commemoration required.
How best to pull it off, how best to weather my duties.

I'll see myself having lunch in silence, my wife
drinking tea while thumbing a new *Titanic* volume.
There's a page of ornate boarding passes, something
about Belfast, a blonde-grey photo of three women.

And this image leaves me gripped by confidence.
Then the dreamt meal is finished, and I'm in Lahardane,
a fiery method woken again in my wrists. I'm half
committee member and half starry conduit of ocean

voices. Slowly, but without inhibition, I work the bell,
convinced the sound is a mounting of better nature
fit to meet what is not life in life, as the April darkness
upholds the thought that the lost are listening now.

HANDBALL LEGEND

Outside the church I heard bits and pieces.
Someone told the story of Jarlath's last day,
how he'd left his sister's house and walked

two miles to the golf course in his pyjamas.
He'd been in bed all the previous month,
her feeding him a bottle a day, no questions.

Someone on the fifth tee had seen Jarlath searching
for balls in the drain off the second fairway.
'He would have done that a lot as a boy,'

someone else said respectfully. 'A golf ball
is a great tool for a hard-as-nails handballer.
Toughens the hands.' The coffin appeared then,

six massive grey brothers bearing it, all of them
weeping. We blessed ourselves, and someone said,
softly, 'Makes *shite* of the hands, more like.'

THE MINK TRAP

Build the trap tonight.
This is mink trap weather.
The county is a sphere of sleet.
Cold animates the cows.
You've three large turkeys,
a pen that was two days work.
Say it. 'Mink are not native.'

You feel closer to your father,
having my threat to curse.
Him perched so awkwardly
beside you on the tractor,
thin legs tight against your arm.
And how my teeth keep you talking,
both of you smoking hard

while fluently denouncing
my river-sponsored attacks.
I love that agricultural face,
the shared squint assessing
costly birds, fear blushing
in the imagination of mink life.
Build the trap tonight.

A fish head, some petrol,
wet cement, a greased pipe, a hole.
And when I am caught,
let my otherworldly voice
infuse the huddled farm.
Your father will say, 'Only
one thing frightens a mink:

the sound of a mink in agony.'
Have it then, the yield of a job

done in the old man's way.
Have your kill, with my thanks,
for mobilising the others,
for freeing my winter heat
from incarnation.

GARDEN GRAFFITI

Before the rains of sight
whipped the foal

of the self into thinking,
and before this world came

pealing and reeling
in fires borrowed

from previous worlds,
I wanted you.

ROOSTER

Whenever I want my six or seven wives to regroup,
to abandon across the farm their dung accountancy,
    I call out.

My emerald mind rattles, my claws clasp firmly
    at the stony yard,
and soon, in twos and threes, they return to the coop.

But why do they come so quickly, clucking in compliance?
Do their jittery souls fill up with some proof of lordship

the instant I negate the day with throaty venting?
I did not choose my authority, the sternness I brandish

so well each day, and there are times when I can only
    doubt it:
quiet mornings when the summer's laws are fractionally
    out,

the light in the mint-anchored presence of the sycamores
seeming almost ready to spill down a truer belonging.

I observe them then, dozing near me, my apprehensive family.
What would it be to attack the morning from this warmth?

I picture my final call. The hens at peace, the trees above,
the dissolving moon, each insisting, 'You are woken life.'

I'll have honed a special curse, a dance to corner the autumn.
I'll be heading to my death, aping the mild earth, and then,

upsetting myself, grief-winged, I'll accost the sun. I'll flare up,
convinced this house of embarrassed girls was holy.

THE GURU

I'm supposed to be working. The accounts are a mess.
But I always go to the office door and cock an ear
when Jack is winding down one of his classes.
No matter how challenging his day might have been
(even in recent weeks, with his marriage unravelling)
and no matter how inspired he may have seemed during
    the class,
his delivery tends to go up a gear at the end.
Jack Gallagher's closing words are always beautiful.

Tonight was special. A pregnancy yoga class.
Ten women in various lulled and swollen states,
kneeling and gently perspiring. Ten pregnant women
opening their hearts to the sound of Jack Gallagher's voice.
He was giving them the breath awareness stuff.
A circulation of hunger came shouldering through
the incense, an arousal that Jack, pacing barefoot,
prompts unwittingly when he's selling meditation.

Wrapping up, he threw in two phrases from his book
(which most of these adoring women have read):
'cultivating the void,' and 'the methods of bliss.'
I'd have complimented him on this after the class,
but it's never like that. There's never the right moment
for friendly remarks with Jack. I've learned this.
You stand there, seduced, but ready to retreat, accepting
from his presence, from the pressure of his gift, your fear.

VISITING MATRON MOORE

Bridie and I were cutting up photos of her husband.
An hour had passed in her kitchen with no word spoken.
There was only the immersion of the work.
And then she said, 'I'm rotten with loneliness.'

I was twelve. This to me was unreasonable candour.
And Bridie must have known. She gulped her cup of wine,
her old face rounding with renewed penance.
Returning to the job, I swept a dozen triangles

of John Moore on his wedding day into a shoebox.
Bridie's queer smile proclaimed my increasing skill.
She cut a picture of two men and two white ponies
into strips, passed them to me, and I cut them smaller.

'He was a great man to handle a yearling,' she said.
'Nearly got himself killed more than a few times.
Other men's sour mares getting all hoorish in sheds
that were too small for horsing in the first place.

Auld relics of cow houses.' She spoke to a photo then.
'You were, Mister. You were foolhardy. But you were
always a great man to get a rope onto a bad animal.'
I possessed no edge for shaming or silencing her.

So I laughed. Anything to stanch this spurt of adult life.
And I was punished. 'You're not concentrating,'
she shouted. 'That's my nursing scissors. Give them here.
There's no surgeon in the world that welcomes a giggler.'

SISTER PATRICK JOSEPH

In her early years, Sister Patrick Joseph
was a figure of fun. More often it was
her eloquence. Mayo farms and towns did not
tend to embrace such things in a plain girl.

Then, at eighteen, a Titanic fare got her
somehow to the States. She ploughed on, in grief,
and found a home in a cult south of Chicago.
But within a month her spirits changed their tack.

She had called the leader, for sport, a 'source
Monger,' thinking it pithy in the sense
that it spoke of peddling soulish notions.
The leader questioned wrongly, 'source mongrel?'
And as she mocked him, coining better taunts,
she knew the editor Jesus owned her mouth.

CULT CORRESPONDENCE

I was strange, and those three months were strange.
And you should know your charisma blunted me,
in body and in soul, so that I can't now

meditate without fearing that I might
trigger into wakefulness new ghosts.
Tonight environmental vows define

my breathing. But neither can I curse
the damage you've done, lest my mind turn
again and lope back to that thick meadow,

to the farm where deep insight and deeper peace
are fed to those, unlike myself, who need it.

To look at them, those two wiry brothers,
passing away slowly in that cosy ward,
quietly confused, imperceptibly pained,
and only when their breaths allow it
resistant to the staff, you'd never imagine
the darkness they brought to my boyhood.
I'd a few Christmas drinks on me last night.
I shouldn't have, but something drove me
to tell the Pilkington story to the nurses.
How, as a boy, my two taciturn uncles
drove me to St Mary's in Castlebar, to pluck
Paddy Pilkington, the gifted handballer,
from the warmth of his psychiatric bed.
'Look at them now in their cots,' I said.
'These two ladeens, you mightn't imagine,
were rogues enough to cajole a doctor
with guilty GAA talk.' I was laughing then,
but no one laughed with me, which was
odd, you know, because the presence
of nurses is itself a classic encouragement.
Not a single half-festive smirk. But I went on:
'Paddy had won the semi-final, had a chance
of winning the thing outright, and was only
re-committed because he'd drank for a week
after his only sister, Mags, died in childbirth.'
My loose tongue was computing pure welcomes
for every phrase here. To my stoney listeners
I said, 'Married name Doyle. Ye might
know the daughters. Larger ladies. You'd see
them maybe in town on Fridays.' I was,
I can admit, full of pints, but not so gone
as not to feel the detail of the sister's death
was the least acceptable shade in my story.
Who was I, in off the street, snow on my shoes,

steering the orbits of cold obstetric comets
onto the bauble-planets of the birth of Christ?
Who was I, working resentful portraits
of two grey-faced patients on Christmas eve?
To quieten me, I'm sure, a young nurse
offered Quality Street. I chose a green one
and went on: 'We drove Paddy up to Dublin,
this pair in the front seat, me and Paddy
in the back. And he won the bloody final.'
I was offered tea then. I'd raised my voice,
picturing that roadside near Mullingar,
the profound cold and dark of the midlands,
the profoundly fearful bird voices in the ditch.
'I'll never forgive them,' I said, taking the tea.
'For driving off. Cowards. Me only nine or ten.
Pilkington having a fit: pure lunatic stuff.
And then he fires his medal at the stars.'

THE REFORMER

I appear off the train at another city, the angel
    of the new medicine.
There is a golden intolerance perched in my eyes.
    My handshake is unearthly.
I describe myself this way, being conscious of how
    I am feared

and not minding if they curse my vision. They are
    bound to curse my vision.
I have tasted grace and I have momentum. The work
    will speak for itself.
I've been closing schools. Last year it was nine: nine swift,
    comprehensive eclipses

of nine charlatan institutions. And this year, since January:
    twenty-two.
Last week, it was a house of gentlemanly homeopaths
    in Illinois
that I shouldered into obscurity, on the grounds of
    their having no library.

They'd hosted me for three days. There was a banquet,
    a tour, some presentations,
and then a day's fishing. That night a woman was wheeled
    in to express miraculous relief
from what seemed to me a position of miraculous
    dependency. She was shaking

so I pretended to be charmed. And this prompted my
    hosts to expect success.
Much extra wine was consumed: the kind of drinking
    that men undertake
when their hearts are transmitting jets of cosmic validity
    up into their brains.

On the last morning, like attentive sons, they escorted me
    to the train,
but then, on hearing my verdict, they wanted the cost
    of their hosting returned.
I gave it to them, and then I offered handshakes.
    One refused. Two of them wept.

Today, a Chicago newspaper reports this scene as
    'an altercation on the railway.'
They've singled out as a particular injustice my partaking
    of the fishing trip,
in the light of my intention to request that the homeopaths
    dissolve their business.

Most Chicago medics would have me strung up in their
    plague-promoting parlours.
To them I'm the Bulldog. Often, with the train lulling me,
    I imagine this contempt.
And I depart from it, into grace, into immunity, into
    a yielding dream of political momentum.

My sleep deepens and the vision of the work rises up,
    speaking for itself, beaming
out from the carriage across a Midwestern blankness:
    O the dance of cutting these cults
from the body of the new curriculum.

Cyrano de Bergerac

I've written a fair few wedding speeches in my time,
mostly for men I don't really know, celebrating brides
    I've never met.
I'd have a bit of a name in the town.

Last night, in Kennedy's kitchen, myself and Kennedy crafted
a few one-liners about his fiancée's people.
For my trouble, he let me smoke, he fed me beer.
    He drank tea himself.

Kennedy's looking forward now to standing up
    at the wedding table, in that furnace of popularity.
If he gets it right, he'll smoothly praise the mother-in-law's
    cooking.
I've left him a few ideas on evoking her worried genius.

He'll go on to tackle the father-in-law's austerity with
    a GAA gibe.
But the issue of the bride's beauty needs some work.
What he described from the heart but unromantically

as 'her focus in life, her diligent nature,' won't do.
'Don't say that,' I said sternly. 'I'll think of something else
and I'll text it to you. Have you a story about the first time
    you met her?

With Kevin Howley's speech, that's what we did,
and it went down a bomb. They can't get enough of that.
    The courtship is key.
Remember, the wedding is the end of the courtship,

so you have to give them a sense of something
    monumentally sweet,
a thing dying and expanding in that very moment.

Speak to create immersion.
The big meal and the dancing are like the great machine

of an absolutely poignant destiny, gastrically oiled,
    fuelled by the sincerity
and daftness of herds of relations. Be aiming for tears.
    Always aim for tears.'
'Feckin hell,' said Kennedy, a man I know to be unfaithful,

'You should go pro with this stuff.' I was embarrassed,
    then vexed.
'Get a bloody website up and running. This is gold,' he said.
While he jotted, I talked, partaking, in my way, as I drank
    the free cans,

of his bride, of their odd, sumptuous joy. I saw myself
    floating into the hotel.
A troop of buxom staff scooping vegetables saw me
    as a colleague.
I said, 'Wedding audiences are a doss.' And Kennedy
    scribbled in his new kitchen.

On leaving, I received fag-money. A fiver and coins: eight
    euro something.
My gift to him was declining my invitation. I staggered
    past his flashy car.
And he knew, I could tell, that lately I'm literally killing
    myself with drink.

Genuinely, I don't know where it comes from.
    The courtship is key?
Gold … And I'm dying in this town. I'm lost.
    I've never had a woman.
But I know there are days that can lift you and cleanse you
    if you're ready.

MOY NURSES

Before I deteriorated, before I entered my final summer,
my neighbours distrusted me. In the evenings I'd stand
smiling in my doorway, listening to the Moy, amused,
though I never expressed it, by how readily the pictures

and predictions came. The humble, elongated decades
had refined, I suppose, my gift for reading the weather
in the trout-convolving voice of the ford at nightfall.
It was in my throat and in my stomach, that apparatus

for receiving and reckoning the elements, the sense
of what the mindless Atlantic might steer onto the farms.
Half a foot in the difference was a world of difference
in the river. If broad black stones were being slathered

uncommonly, in currents fed by darker, less coastal skies,
if a skullish rock ensconced in spilling hills was arguing,
then, in mutual possession, I heard it. Gradient, drainage,
alluvium: here I had fluency. It was a kind of child's play,

my quiet brain ladling out her stock of exacting dreams.
But I had to be weak before the village embraced them.
For my uncanny ways to appear harmless, I had to be sick.
In my last weeks, several local daughters were appointed

my river-chaperones. Where before I had disturbed them,
now on warm days, without fail, buoyant girls collected me
and led me down to where the Moy was running lower
than in living memory and more quiet. They brought their

homework, or bits of sewing; they put cake in my slack gob.
The mind of the water was held in cloud on my final day.

I went heavily to my knees. But when the Reddington sisters placed their hands on my back, one telling the other to run

for their father, a fund of life rose clear and deep to take me.

.

The pike swims under the otter, and the otter dives
    into the moon,
and the moon grows young with the unfound girls forever.

The fundraiser's handbook gives it to you straight.
Rule Number One: *Be bullish with your inspiration.*
With the bigger events, you'll always be laughed at.
But they have to laugh. This is wide-spread generosity
we're talking about: the most abundant element
and the least available. Laugh with them, and plough on.
The initial response must always be ignored.
Behind the trees, inside the hills of the initial response,
that is where the cave of warm donations lies.
Rule Number One: *Be bullish with your inspiration.*

The pike swims under the otter, and the otter dives
    into the moon,
and the moon grows young with the unfound girls forever.

Rule Number Two: *Hold this like the body of a lover
in your mind's eye: wide-spread generosity,
wide-spread generosity.* When it's a water safety gig,
believe that the names of the rivers involve every
human life. Imagine the search and recovery man
as the patron saint of those blunt, mid-forties drinkers
who once were diamonds in the scouts. Believe
if you enter a pub, armed only with a white bucket,
chanting: 'Moy, Pontoon and Gweestion, Moy,
Pontoon and Gweestion,' with this as your only message,

that still you'll be showered with coins, because
the idea of rivers, well put, corners a man's nerves,
prods the core of his apathy and prods his boyhood,
until he's pledging his support, digging deep at the bar,

suddenly hit by the knowledge of the cold search,
and the cold recovery, and reckoning then in his gut
that the search and recovery man is the patron saint
of the life-buoyancy of selflessness. Rule Number Two:
Hold this like the body of a lover in your mind's eye:
wide-spread generosity, wide-spread generosity.

The pike swims under the otter, and the otter dives
    into the moon,
and the moon grows young with the unfound girls forever.

Rule Number Three: *As if your life depended on it,*
have mugs and t-shirts printed. The search and recovery man
is the patron saint of fresh clothes and hot, sweet tea.
Absorb an image of the men that crawl in black currents,
prodding at muck, asking the swollen river, 'Where
have you taken the piece of life we cannot hope
you'll respect, River, snake-mirrored, stone-stomached,
self-tunnelling River. Where is the memorial woman
you've held since the old bridge, straddling you, dropped
    her?'
When it's a water safety gig, include this spirit,

coil it into a logo for the merchandise, with the green
angel of the bulrush and the red angel of the raft.
When wide-spread generosity is woken between the towns,
and a crowd goes down to the river (alive to the notion
that the search and recovery man is the patron saint
of women giving birth to hundreds of sandwiches at the
    drop of a hat),
give them something to wear and something to drink from.
The logo will bloom when the canoeists are paddling
against the tug of the loss that has prompted your vision
and called you to live by Rule Number Three:

As if your life depended on it, have mugs and t-shirts printed.

The pike swims under the otter, and the otter dives
    into the moon,
and the moon grows young with the unfound girls forever.

The pike swims under the otter, and the otter dives
    into the moon,
and the moon grows young with the unfound girls forever.

When she met him in Swinford, touching his famous hand,
she could not have known the desire within his silence,
could not have guessed her own influence, her care-free voice
entering him, planting visions in his sleepless future.

Nor, as she wheeled the harp to her father's banquet table,
that their blind guest might conjure an imageless beauty,
could she have imagined O'Carolan committing to memory,
so minutely, the coast-whispers of her gown.

Far from the simplicity of her youth was the musician's
     hunger,
far his porter-wet beard, his bed of frozen grass crackling
under a bodhrán moon. Far too his final night, that old
     fondness
almost quenching the apparition: *Her, the Brabazon waneen,*

approaching him across a field, like the field's intention;
picking the tether of his mind from the earth, standing
     over him;
rousing with her laughter the voles in their nettle baskets
and prompting the near-dead harper to speak to the
     darkness.

WILD SALMON

Wild salmon, that's what Peter used to call
    the Charlestown girls,
the few that would appear in the small pub a few times
    a year.
And just as we couldn't keep up with him in his swift
    drinking,

we could never hope to match his handling of these visitors.
The clear-headed lust, the primal strategy when two high
    heels
approached the bar to order drinks. Not physically
    'handling' them,

never that, though his face offered an unkind hunger,
    part heartbreak,
part loquacious, vaguely forgivable lechery. But handling
    them
with congeniality, with lippy, aimless friendship.
    And they'd respond,

smiling the smiles of women who've never dreamed
    so much craic
could be stirred by their arrival. The smile
    of unaccustomed glamour.
Thick make-up glowed in the glare of Peter's wit
    and his implication,

somehow sharper in the act of rolling a cigarette while
    talking: 'Listen girl,
a man has chosen you from the gaggle that climbed from
    that taxi
in the eternal rain of this dying town an hour ago.
    You've earned his heat,

his admiration. And you can glance back at your friends
    all you like
instead of replying; but I have you, haven't I? While
    the younger lads here,
your shyer, more likely wooers, skull pints in the shadow
    of my craft.'

ANNUNCIATIONS

Every time I call the security company, I get a different
    group of lads.
Rough Dubs, hard as you like, young and usually chatty.
    This can cause
awkwardness going from Dublin down to Knock.
    Typically, they'll think
a clairvoyant is a gas thing. And that the Knock job is a gas
    kind of job.

And they'll challenge me eventually, one of them insisting
    I'll have earned
their undying admiration if I'll admit that my work, my
    reported earnings,
and most of all my success in Knock, are all based on a gift
    for shite-talk.
They're riveted then when I speak of the thousands who'll
    always travel

on the appointed dates, the simple shrine turned cosmic
    again at my say-so.
They're tickled by the image of parents thrusting semi-
    conscious children
upon me, and the daft donations shoved into my pockets.
    Hordes of believers,
desperately convinced, immune in fact to any sort of doubt.
    Deliberately,

on nearing Mayo, I regale my bodyguards with these
    stories of the devout.
It primes them, I find, for what can be a cold and obscure
    weekend's graft.
But when they grow pushy on the issue of my visions, I
    ignore the slagging.

You'll have heard it yourself, Mary, that garrulous
    inability to comprehend

the truth of what you and I have by way of a dialogue,
    by way of a contract.
If I were to tell them about the bath, that first evening
    that you visited me,
your slick dive through the planets, through the roof
    of my hallucinations,
the water around my teenage body getting hot;
    or how you conjured an image,

something from Easter, a reflective sycamore and a dark
    cloud of starlings,
and how this fed my grasp of your grief, your scope, Mary,
    and your wish to visit.
And then, as I knelt, woken from my life, quietly praying,
    a deep strangeness
without distress took hold, and I sensed on your robes
    my calling's spoor ...

But if for a moment any of this, my queen, seems worth
    sharing, if I imagine
it might prove palatable to the henchmen assembled
    for our special day, I stop.
They're on board, they're fond of me, and you, vast virgin,
    are in their lives again.
I'll put on the air of an employer. I'll ask them
    if it's their first trip to the West.

EQUINE THERAPY

Sam's father keeps gin in his car.
He has an eye on the riding lesson
but mostly he reads his paper and drinks.
His daughter is struggling. She doesn't
absorb what we pretend we're offering:
a second mind, a supplementary life-force.

The illness perched in Sam's personality
outmanoeuvres the games we play in the saddle.
It blanks the vast neutrality gathered
in the being of the horse. After the class
tonight I told her dad that my mares,
my *ladies*, are focussed, that they're mute

professionals of the highest order.
His face showed calm inconsolability
and he spoke from his place in life, ward
of this mordantly promiscuous girl,
unreachable in the backseat of his car,
compliant this time, but not content,

plainly immune to novel interventions.
I wanted to say the horses will nail it,
in time, that this is only the second week.
We should trust the grey. She's begun
to intuit the constriction, the hampered light
in the core of the cowed young rider.

I know by her. Tonight, as she feeds
she'll be hoping her new client's brain
will decelerate, lulled by a presence
unrousable without trotting. I could've
said: the burdens that burn us are contrived
by the cosmos to draw us here, into the clinic

of the wild. But lately I don't believe it,
although I'm fond of saying it, and though
a jargony, more detached version of that credo
is what seals my trickle of State funding.
How could I say that I've seen too many
like him, that my expert work is improvised,

subtle, impacting, and heartening as it is,
that there are days I seek to cut with my love alone
the unkind roots that live in these children,
or that there are nights I go to the stables,
view my glowing team where they rest,
and deem them cruel for wasting their boundless hearts?

Rip Van Winkle

Last month, when I left
the office, I recall
it was bucketing rain.

I'd had my coffee,
my crisps, my sandwich
from the petrol station.

There was every reason
to think I would return.
Nothing in my mood

spoke a readiness
to be off marrying the land
in some special cave,

or finding incredible rest
through the charm
of the drenched roads.

But off I went, to where
the edge of town
declared a huddled life,

a sense of patient beasts
arranged for miles.
Yet still no hint of wild

absorption and release.
To think the names
of the nearby fishing spots

was to know only
the gentle shame
of an unsuitable footwear.

Loosening my tie
and breathing brought only
the disregard of grasses.

More the fortune then
that I am, some weeks now,
lost in a wealth

of sources that combine
the hawthorn's claws
with the sun, lost

within this pasture's
flashing, this clear
September face that laps,

unflagging, the hub
of the governing wren.
But what is this life-force

mistressing my lunch hour,
hewing with water
the cause of my descent?

And what am I if I dwell
in transformation,
if the thrust of waiting

prolongs this change,
masks me in light,
dogs me nightly with wonder?

THE MADNESS OF KING GOLL

Mother was from Kerry.
That is why I am running
through these wet nights,
across a soaked Connacht.

Unclothed, I hide in the day,
listening to the rough land's
notion: 'Kerry will calm you.'
Cold, maternal Kerry,

place of breath-sponsoring dunes,
in whose tough grasses
loud ocean light will cool
the old argument that has

captained all too often
this old brain, a brain Mother
once said was straight out
of Father's people. Another

night of exertion, then,
lured on, hiking to asylum,
renouncing other counties
(Roscommon, Mayo, Galway),

another night of Mother's rain
mouthing into Father's spirit,
another night hunting a dawn
to crown the loss of the North.

TEA WITH A SILAGE QUEEN

With your young arm wedged into this old bale of hay
you could reach for the heart of the shed itself.
And know a special moisture there,
a rude seepage mouthlessly kissing your hand.

It is not in the agricultural books
but there is a grade of wonder that the shed detects.
Some boys will lose a month here,
their brains bound in ecstasy, their jaws

set in a vulva-consciousness of meadows.
They're not much company then, I can tell you,
crouching and shaking, stabbing at their dream of storage,
thinking themselves elected to a massive harmony,

and somehow summoned to the inner life of fields,
whose cause, you know, is not the ratty root
of the farm itself, but a root of seasons
which only I have known.

THE BADGER

Go out, good son, head off across the hill,
in dripping hood, with lewd nocturnal eye.

Go out and slouch across the walls of dawn,
all aptitude and bluebell pride and tooth.

Go out, my son, and stave a whitethorn beast
by ancestral grin and doggedness in rain.

Defy, my son, the pasture, the imperial sheds;
with nettle mind, defy the piercing town.

And when by farming, son, the farms are lost,
and tangled night becomes a badger throne,

then restore, my fattened son, the digging way,
unlatch the earth, release your father's bones.

THE SILENT MAN
For John and Ginny Stamler

Here is the house of the silent man.
This tree was his personal oak.

He lived for love, and he passed love on,
and yet he seldom spoke.

A number of these poems, or versions of them, were originally published in the following places: *Poetry Ireland Review*, *The Irish Times*, *The Cork Literary Review*, *Cyphers*, *The John McGahern Yearbook*, *ROPES*, *The Stinging Fly*, *The Oxford Magazine*, *College Green*, *Icarus*, *The Moth*, *Earthlines*.

'Huckleberry Finn Day' has been published as a limited edition chapbook by the International Writing Program at the University of Iowa.

A handwritten version of 'Turlough O'Carolan at Brabazon House' has been installed as part of the Healing Word exhibit at Mayo General Hospital.

'The Timoney Bell', 'The Reformer' and 'Huckleberry Finn Day' began their lives as commissioned poems. Thanks are due to the Addergoole Titanic Society, the Education Division in the School of Medicine at Trinity College Dublin, and the founders of Huckleberry Finn Day, all of whom provided special subjects and special occasions for first readings. 'The Reformer' is based on historical impressions of the American educationalist Abraham Flexner (1866–1959).

The author wishes to thank Dublin UNESCO City of Literature, the Department of Arts, Heritage and the Gaeltacht, the Arts Council, and Culture Ireland, for their support during his time at the University of Iowa in 2013 and 2014.